INTO DEEP SPACE

PAUL VIRR

CARLTON KiDS

WELCOME TO THE UNIVERSE

The story of the Universe begins in the night sky. Light from the stars has travelled from so far away that it has taken many thousands of years to reach us. So, when we gaze at the stars, we are looking back through time. These distant observations give us clues about how and when the Universe began.

0 TO 5 SECONDS
13.7 billion years ago, the Universe expands in the Big Bang. Matter, energy, space and time are all instantly created, as are forces such as gravity and the electromagnetic force.

380,000 YEARS
The first atoms form. Light is given out by matter and the Universe becomes transparent (as light can travel through the vacuum of space).

9 BILLION YEARS
Our Solar System is forming.

3 MINUTES
At this stage, and for around 380,000 years after the Big Bang, the Universe is too hot for atoms to be stable or for light to shine.

200 MILLION YEARS
The first stars and galaxies begin to form from gases concentrated (brought together) by gravity.

13.7 BILLION YEARS
The Universe continues to expand, faster than ev[...]

THE BIG BANG

The Universe is the whole of space and everything in it – the Earth, our Solar System and our galaxy the Milky Way, plus billions of other galaxies, stars and planets. We think that the Universe began around 13.7 billion years ago with a colossal explosion, the Big Bang. Before this event, all the raw materials of the Universe were concentrated into a super-dense and super-hot space, which was smaller than an atom. This suddenly expanded, creating space, matter, energy and time – everywhere – at the same moment.

From its orbit around the Earth, the Hubble Space Telescope has captured images of some of the most dis[...] objects in the observable Unive[...]

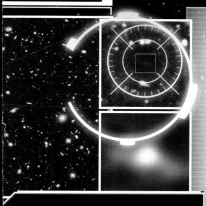

SHAPING THE UNIVERSE

After the Big Bang, the expansion of the Universe kept going – and as it spread out, it cooled. About 380,000 years later, the cooling temperatures slowed the tiny particles that made up the Universe enough for them to combine and form the first stable atoms. Gravity, the force of attraction between objects with mass, then gradually began to shape the Universe. Over millions of years, the scattered matter of the Universe began to concentrate into forms that we recognize today. Vast clouds of hydrogen gas became denser and began to burn, forming stars. Gravity pulled these stars together to form galaxies. The galaxies, too, were drawn together to form galaxy clusters and superclusters, eventually forming a colossal network of galaxies that stretches throughout the Universe.

The first stars burst into brightness about 200 million years after the Big Bang. The red dot in the centre of the image on the right above, from the Hubble Space Telescope, shows a mini-galaxy that is one of the oldest found so far.

This Hubble image shows evidence of dark matter around a galaxy cluster known as CL0024+17.

THE DARK SIDE OF THE UNIVERSE

There are more forces at work in the Universe than we can directly measure. In fact, all the stars, galaxies, black holes, nebulae and everything else we know about in space may make up just four per cent of the Universe. The rest is made from two mysterious parts: an invisible type of matter called dark matter (23 per cent of the Universe) and a strange force called dark energy (which makes up the remaining 73 per cent).

All things, from atoms to galaxies, are affected by gravity – including Andromeda, our closest neighbouring galaxy.

THE EARLY UNIVERSE

The intense heat and energy created by the Big Bang left a dying afterglow behind, known as the Cosmic Microwave Background Radiation (or CMBR). Specialized space telescopes have been launched into orbit to measure it. The Planck spacecraft, for example, is so sensitive that it can detect temperature differences of just a few millionths of a degree. The CMBR information it has collected has been used to create a temperature map of the sky, showing the tiny differences in temperature from the start of the Universe. The cold spots reveal where the greatest density of matter is, and show that the shape of the Universe is fairly flat.

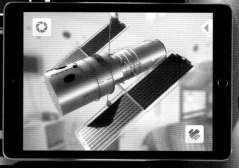

iEXPLORE

HUBBLE TELESCOPE

Use your app to get up-close to the Hubble Space Telescope in amazing 3D. Tap the button to reveal an X-ray view!

THE SOLAR SYSTEM:
OUR HOME IN SPACE

Our planet, Earth, is where we have to start from when we try to work out our place in the Universe. Over the centuries, we have explored deeper and deeper into space. From the observations of early astronomers to the development of space telescopes, probes and robotic landers, we continue to expand the frontiers of our knowledge across the vast distances of space. But the place we know most about is the region around the Sun, the star that we orbit. This is the Solar System, our home in space.

Saturn

Jupiter

Mars

Sun

Mercury

THE EMPIRE OF THE SUN

The Solar System consists of all the objects held by the pull of gravity from its central star – the Sun. This includes eight planets that orbit the Sun, plus all the dwarf planets, asteroids, comets and the scattered dust, debris and gas in between. The Sun makes up 99.9 per cent of the mass of the Solar System, which is why its gravity makes it the central point around which everything turns. The planets occupy an area that stretches up to 6 billion km from the Sun, but the whole Solar System measures about two light years – or 19,000 billion km – across.

ORBITING THE SUN

Each planet has its own oval orbit around the Sun, with the inner planets moving faster than the outer planets. The Earth is the third planet from the Sun. Travelling at 108,000 km/h, it takes just over 365 days, an Earth year, to complete one orbit. The dwarf planet Pluto, travelling on the distant outskirts of the Solar System, takes more than 248 Earth years to complete its orbit.

Pluto

Neptune

Uranus

Venus

Earth

BRIGHT PLANETS

In the night sky, the planets seem to outshine many of the stars. However, unlike stars, planets do not produce any light of their own. It is the reflection of the Sun's light that makes them bright. The planets are vastly smaller than stars. They only appear to be roughly the same size as distant stars because they are much closer to the Earth.

iEXPLORE

SOLAR SYSTEM

Discover and compare the sizes of the Sun and the planets of our Solar System. Tap each planet to move to the next view.

THE INNER PLANETS

The four planets closest to the Sun, made from rock and metal, are known as terrestrial planets. They have solid surfaces and atmospheres of differing gases and thicknesses. These planets have been shaped by powerful geological forces, such as volcanic eruptions, and their surfaces bear the scars of impacts from meteorites.

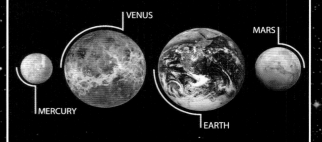

VENUS

MARS

MERCURY

EARTH

THE OUTER PLANETS

Beyond the asteroid belt are four outer planets. They are very large in comparison to the inner planets. More than 1,000 Earths could fit into Jupiter, the largest planet in the Solar System. Like the other outer planets, this giant world is largely made up of gas, with a small core of rock, metals and frozen liquid at the centre. Each of the outer planets has a stormy atmosphere of gases, as well as many moons and a system of rings (made up of small rock or ice particles) around it.

SATURN

NEPTUNE

JUPITER

URANUS

THE SUN:
OUR NEAREST STAR

On a clear night, the sky is filled with thousands of tiny, twinkling stars. Each one is a faraway sun and its light has crossed unimaginable distances to reach us. However, by day there's only one star of the show: the Sun. It's our nearest star, so close that it outshines all the other, more distant stars.

AN AVERAGE STAR

Stars are huge, ever-changing spheres of super-compressed (squeezed) and super-hot gases. The Sun belongs to the most common family of stars in the Universe, known as main sequence stars. These stars are all at a steady, stable phase in their life cycle, during which they radiate energy and light from nuclear reactions taking place in their core. Around 90 per cent of the stars in the known Universe are main sequence stars. Our Sun is a main sequence star of average size, about halfway through its life. It's just one of hundreds of billions of stars in our galaxy, the Milky Way.

The corona is the outermost part of the Sun's atmosphere, which is actually hotter than the layer below it, reaching temperatures of almost 2,000,000°C.

The photosphere is the visible outer surface of the Sun – a thin layer of boiling gases measuring about 100 km thick, with a temperature of about 6,000°C.

MAKING SUNSHINE

The nuclear reactions raging at the centre of the Sun use hydrogen as a fuel, turning it into helium and releasing vast amounts of heat and light energy. At the core, 600 million tonnes of hydrogen are turned into helium each second. The energy this generates can take up to a million years to be transferred through the Sun to the surface. From here, light waves take about eight minutes to travel through space to reach Earth. Light and heat from the Sun have provided the energy that has made life on Earth possible.

The convective zone is the stormy outer layer of the Sun's interior and is about 200,000 km thick. Currents of hot, rising gas and cooler, falling gas transfer energy to the surface. The deepest part of this region has a temperature of about 2,000,000°C.

Sun spots are cooler areas of the photosphere, created by magnetic fields. They look darker and appear and disappear in a cycle that lasts eleven years.

The core is more than a third of the Sun's mass but just one per cent of its volume. The incredible heat and pressure at the core cause atoms to fuse together. This creates huge amounts of energy. The temperature of the core is about 15,000,000°C.

The radiative zone lies between the core and the Sun's outer layers, making up most of the Sun's interior. Energy from the core travels through this zone as particles called photons. Temperatures here reach 8,000,000°C.

The chromosphere is an uneven layer of gas, with temperatures that vary from 6,000°C at the bottom to 20,000°C higher up. It is ever-changing – clouds of gas called prominences arch up into the corona, while gas jets known as spicules can leap 10,000 km above the chromosphere.

SUN FACTS

AGE
Around 4,550 million years old, about halfway through ts lifespan.

SIZE
About 1.4 million km in diameter, more than a hundred times that of Earth.

VOLUME
A million planet Earths could fit into the Sun.

DISTANCE
150 million km from Earth.

COMPOSITION
Around 90 per cent of the Sun is hydrogen gas. The rest is mainly helium gas. Other elements make up less than one per cent.

ROTATION
The Sun does not rotate like a solid ball. Some parts spin faster than others. For example, it takes 25 days for its equator to make one full turn, and 38 days for the regions around the Sun's poles to rotate once.

LOCATION
The centre of our Solar System, and 25,000 light years from the centre of our galaxy.

COMETS AND ASTEROIDS

The enormous pull of the Sun's gravity is what holds our Solar System together. As well as the large spherical planets, millions of much smaller space rocks are held in orbit. These lumps of rock and metal come in many shapes and sizes and are known as asteroids.

Ceres was the first object in the asteroid belt to be found, but it is no longer called an asteroid. Like Pluto, it is now described as a dwarf planet because of its mass and roughly spherical shape.

ASTEROIDS

Asteroids are the debris left over from when the Solar System was formed. Made of metal and rock, they are the fragments that gravity failed to pull together to form planets. Instead, they are trapped in orbit around the Sun. Most asteroids are found in a large, doughnut-shaped area between Mars and Jupiter, known as the asteroid belt. About 200,000 asteroids have been discovered there, but there could be billions more. As they travel around the Sun, asteroids sometimes collide, smashing each other into even smaller bits of rocky debris.

In 2005, the Japanese probe Hayabusa landed on an asteroid called Itokawa. Samples collected by the probe showed Itokawa was made from the same material as stony meteorites.

SIZE AND SHAPE

Most asteroids are the size of boulders, but there are at least 100,000 that measure 20 km across, and more than a hundred are 200 km in diameter. The more massive an asteroid is, the more its gravity is able to mould it into a more spherical shape. Vesta is a flattened ball that makes up nine per cent of the total mass of the asteroid belt. Measuring more than 500 km across, its surface is covered with impact craters. Other massive asteroids are more irregular. Eros is a potato-shaped asteroid measuring 34 km across.

COMETS

Comets have a central nucleus of rocky debris set in frozen liquid. Heat from the Sun releases gas and dust from these icy balls as their orbit brings them closer. This creates a bright, fuzzy cloud – called the coma – around the comet's nucleus, as well as a sunlit trail of gas and dust particles called the tail. The tail can stretch up to 100 million km behind the coma. Comets have large, stretched, oval orbits and some travel for hundreds of thousands of years before passing close to the Earth. If the particles of dust from a comet reach our atmosphere, they burn up as a meteor shower.

While the nucleus of a comet might be up to 10 km across, its coma of dust and gases can be up to a million km across.

On 15 February 2013, a near-Earth asteroid weighing about 12,000 tonnes entered the Earth's atmosphere over Chelyabinsk, Russia. It streaked across the sky as a giant fireball, before exploding 30 km above the ground.

METEORS AND METEORITES

Bright streaks of light, which dart straight across the night sky, are often called shooting stars. However, these fiery trails are actually meteors – small space rocks burning up, due to heat generated by friction, as they travel through Earth's atmosphere. Some meteors do not burn up completely and hit the Earth's surface. These are known as meteorites. They are the solid remains of asteroids or (more rarely) debris from comets, planets or moons.

NEAR-EARTH ASTEROIDS

Most asteroids follow oval-shaped orbits around the Sun, inside the asteroid belt, but some have orbits that take them outside the belt. A large number, called Trojans, orbit at the same distance as Jupiter. Other groups have orbits in the inner Solar System, which can bring them close to Earth. There are nearly 13,000 near-Earth asteroids, which are closely monitored by astronomers. A collision with a large asteroid could be a disaster for our planet.

iEXPLORE

SPACE LANDER

Use the red button to control your space probe and land safely on an asteroid outside our Solar System! Watch for the green safe-zone and your speed on the left.

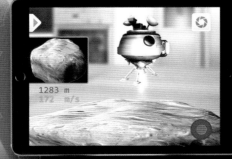

1283 m
172 m/s

010011010101010

OUR GALAXY: THE MILKY WAY

Our Sun and its orbiting planets are just a tiny part of a vast system called a galaxy. Our galaxy is known as the Milky Way. It is a huge, spiralling disc of billions of stars, with countless planets, moons and gigantic clouds of dust and gas all spinning around together.

Scutum-Centaurus Arm

Norma Arm

Orion Spur

Sun

At night, a large fuzzy band of light stretches across the sky. This is how a view towards the centre of the Milky Way appears from Earth, positioned on one of the galaxy's smaller spiral arms.

The Milky Way is about 13.6 billion years old. Some of its oldest stars are likely to be as old as the Universe itself.

OUR PLACE IN THE MILKY WAY

Our Sun and its Solar System are about 25,000 light years from the centre of the Milky Way. If we could zoom out to view our galaxy from space, we would see a bright, central nucleus with curved arms spiralling out from it. These arms are areas of younger, brighter stars. The darker parts between the arms contain fainter stars and huge clouds of gas and dust.

A SPINNING SPIRAL

The Milky Way contains between 200 and 400 billion stars. Its disc spans 100,000 light years from side to side but is only a few thousand light years thick. At the centre is a supermassive black hole, a dense concentration of mass that seems to form the nucleus of most galaxies. The Milky Way spins around this central hub, with our Sun and Solar System orbiting it at a speed of approximately 800,000 km/h. It takes the Sun about 225–250 million years to complete one full orbit of the centre of the galaxy.

A DARK HALO

Just as it holds the Solar System together, gravity also binds the Milky Way into one swirling mass. Surrounding the centre of the galaxy is a bulge, about 10,000 light years in diameter, that contains an enormous amount of tightly packed stars, gas and dust. Gravity is weaker at the galaxy's edges, where it thins into gas clouds.

Surrounding the central bulge, is a ball-shaped halo of older stars, which includes about 200 spherical groupings of stars called globular clusters. There are no dust or gas clouds in the halo, and fewer stars than in the rest of the Milky Way. Scientists think the halo might be part of a giant sphere of dark matter in which the entire galaxy is embedded. At least 90 per cent of the mass of our galaxy could be dark matter. The gravitational forces of this mysterious, invisible matter could be helping to hold the galaxy together.

The bulge of stars at the core of the Milky Way includes star clusters, such as the Arches Cluster, which is 100 light years from the centre. Among the stars at the centre are about 135 huge and incredibly hot young stars, all much larger than our Sun.

Outer Arm

Sagittarius Arm

Perseus Arm

Eta Carinae is one of the most luminous star systems in the Milky Way. It is almost five million times brighter than the Sun.

COSMIC ZOOM

Fly through the Universe with this amazing 360° view! Press the button to move forwards or in reverse and zoom closer or further away from Earth.

iEXPLORE

OTHER WORLDS: EXOPLANETS

Earth is one of eight planets orbiting the Sun. Outside our Solar System, moving around the hundreds of billions of stars in the Milky Way and beyond, there are likely to be billions of other planets. These distant worlds are known as exoplanets.

Some exoplanets, such as Kepler-452b, orbit at a similar distance from their star as the Earth does from our Sun. This suggests that it might be possible for life to exist there.

IN SEARCH OF NEW WORLDS

For thousands of years, astronomers could only imagine that exoplanets existed. It was very likely that distant stars were at the centre of their own solar systems, with planets orbiting them, but such faraway planets were impossible to detect. However, with the development of new technology, the search for other worlds was able to begin. In 1992, three planets orbiting a dead star – called a pulsar – were found. Then, in 1995, the discovery of an exoplanet orbiting a living, Sun-like star was announced. Named 51 Pegasi b, this alien world was only the first of more than 1,900 exoplanets that have since been discovered.

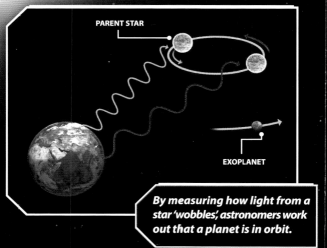

PARENT STAR

EXOPLANET

By measuring how light from a star 'wobbles', astronomers work out that a planet is in orbit.

 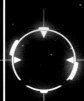

51 Pegasi b is a hot planet about half the size of Jupiter. This gas giant orbits so close to its parent star that a year on the planet (the time it takes to orbit the star) lasts just under 4.5 Earth days.

EXOPLANET SPOTTING

Exoplanets are too far away for even our most powerful telescopes to spot directly. However, sensitive instruments allow scientists to detect the presence of exoplanets by revealing the effect that they have on light from the stars they orbit. An exoplanet can give itself away as it passes in front of a parent star, causing the brightness of the star to decrease. The gravity of an exoplanet can also affect the movement of a star, causing it to travel in a small, circular orbit of its own. The star then appears to wobble, changing the light it gives off towards Earth.

KEPLER-452B – ANOTHER EARTH?

In July 2015, NASA unveiled the discovery of Kepler-452b, an exoplanet in the habitable zone of a star that is similar in size and temperature to our Sun, although it is 1.5 billion years older. Kepler-452b is about 60 per cent larger than Earth, but is small enough to suggest that it is a rocky planet rather than a gas giant. This makes the planet the closest match to Earth discovered so far. However, nobody can be certain that it has liquid water or the other conditions required for life.

Launched in 2009, the Kepler Mission features a space telescope equipped with light-sensors that monitor the brightness of stars. Having found over 2,300 confirmed exoplanets, Kepler has been searching for smaller, Earth-like exoplanets.

This is an artist's impression of Kepler-452b – the exoplanet most likely (so far) to be a candidate for 'Earth 2.0'.

KEPLER-452B

LOCATION
1,400 light years away in the constellation of Cygnus.

SIZE
60 per cent larger than Earth.

GRAVITY
With five times the mass of the Earth, Kepler-452b is thought to have double the gravity of Earth. You'd feel twice as heavy there.

ORBIT
Takes 385 Earth days to orbit its parent star.

SUN
Six billion years old, a main sequence star with a similar mass and temperature to our Sun.

EXOPLANET EXPLORER

Use the button to drive an exoplanet explorer vehicle around your room.

iEXPLORE

GALAXIES: THE BUILDING BLOCKS OF THE UNIVERSE

The Milky Way is one of more than 100 billion galaxies in the Universe. The huge clusters of matter that make up these other, distant galaxies are so far away that we couldn't see them until the 1920s. The development of powerful telescopes and the work of astronomers such as Edwin Hubble meant that individual stars could finally be picked out from fuzzy blurs of light. Today, we also know how these galaxies move and interact, joining together to give large-scale structure to the Universe.

DIFFERENT SHAPES AND SIZES

The hundreds of millions of stars in our own Milky Way are joined together in a barred-spiral shape. But this is not the only type of galaxy in the Universe. In fact, spiral-shaped galaxies probably make up just over a quarter of the galaxies we know about, while galaxies said to be dwarf elliptical are the most common. These are much smaller, containing just a few million stars held together in a roughly spherical shape.

The Large and Small Magellanic Clouds are dwarf irregular galaxies. They form part of a group of galaxies clustered near to the Milky Way.

NGC 6872 is a barred-spiral galaxy, five times larger than the Milky Way. Its large spiral arms form a vast diameter of 522,000 light years. It is thought to contain hundreds of billions of stars.

Astronomers have broadly classified galaxies as having one of three basic shapes: spiral, elliptical and irregular. But there are many examples that blur the boundaries between these shapes. It may be that the different shapes represent different stages of a galaxy's development, rather than being the result of the different ways in which the galaxies originally formed.

SPIRAL GALAXIES

A spiral galaxy is a slowly rotating disc of stars with a bright, spiral-shaped pattern. It has a central bulge and is surrounded by a large, spherical halo. The bulge and halo are mostly made up of older stars, while the curved arms of the spiral contain the youngest, brightest stars. These stars are so hot that they burn with a white or blue colour. New stars are created at the leading edges of the arms, whose motion leads to their formation from the interstellar gas and dust within the disc. About two-thirds of spiral galaxies are barred spirals – like our Milky Way – with an elongated, bar-shaped region in the centre.

ELLIPTICAL GALAXIES

Elliptical galaxies mainly consist of older, less bright stars. Unlike spiral galaxies, they do not have nebulae (with molecular clouds of gas or dust) with which to make new stars. Larger elliptical galaxies are perfectly spherical, while smaller ones are more elongated. Like spirals, they are surrounded by a halo of dark matter and spherical clusters of stars. Ellipticals include some of the largest and smallest galaxies in the Universe.

LENTICULAR AND IRREGULAR GALAXIES

Lenticular galaxies are lens-shaped, with a rounded nucleus and a disc of stars. They don't have spiralling arms of young stars or interstellar clouds of gas for making new stars. Irregular galaxies appear to have even less structure. They look like great waves or clouds of stars, or misshapen versions of other galaxy types. Irregulars have a mix of older and younger stars, plus clouds of gas and dust.

GALAXY CLUSTERS

Galaxies of every type are spread unevenly throughout the Universe, but they are not independent of each other. Thanks to gravity, their movements through space bring them together in pairs, groups or clusters. Between the clusters are thin clouds of hydrogen gas and dark matter. This is known as the intergalactic medium. Galaxy clusters go on to form superclusters, creating vast, branching chains that make up the largest known structures of the Universe.

EVOLVING AND COLLIDING
GALAXIES

Galaxies are classified according to their shape in the Hubble Sequence diagram below.

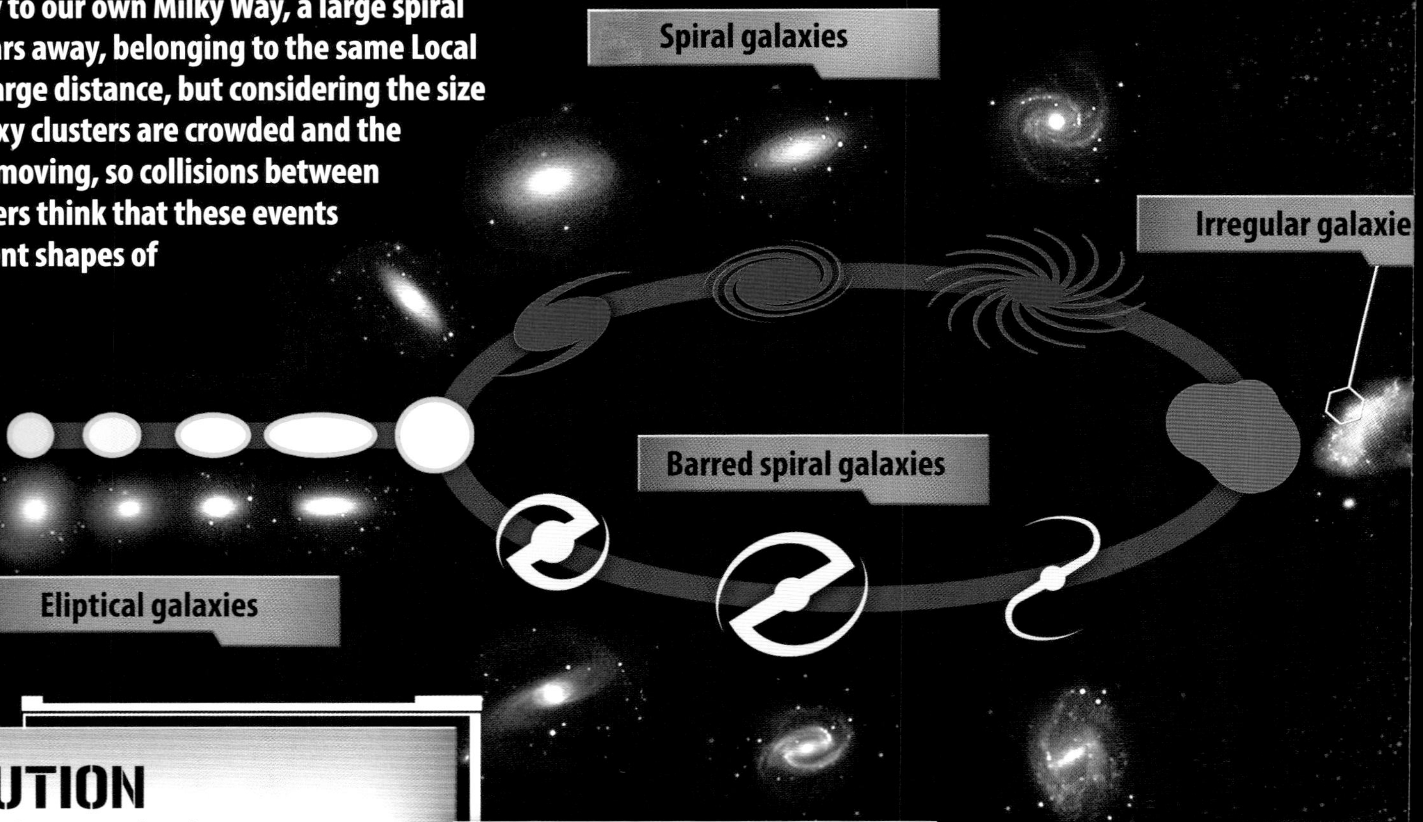

Andromeda is the nearest galaxy to our own Milky Way, a large spiral galaxy some 2.2 million light years away, belonging to the same Local Group cluster. This seems like a large distance, but considering the size of galaxies, it is quite close. Galaxy clusters are crowded and the galaxies inside them are always moving, so collisions between galaxies are common. Astronomers think that these events may be the reason for the different shapes of galaxies found in the Universe.

Spiral galaxies

Irregular galaxie

Barred spiral galaxies

Eliptical galaxies

GALACTIC EVOLUTION

One theory about how galaxies formed suggests that they condensed from vast clouds of matter, forming stars as a part of this process. However, the presence of ancient stars and black holes – things that must have been created shortly after the Big Bang – makes it more likely that galaxy formation started with stars. The stars drew together to form irregular galaxies, which then evolved into spiral galaxies, and elliptical galaxies. This pattern of development is supported by our observations of distant galaxies. These show that, in the earlier stages of the Universe, there were a larger proportion of smaller, irregular galaxies than there are now.

The Large Magellanic Cloud is a satellite galaxy that orbits the Milky Way. It now appears to be an irregular galaxy, but the bar-shaped concentration at its centre suggests that it was once a barred-spiral galaxy. The gravitational forces of the Milky Way may have disrupted its shape and dispersed its spiral arms.

INTERACTING GALAXIES

How galaxies change (evolve), through collisions or the effect of the gravity of nearby galaxies, depends on many factors – such as how close the different galaxies get, their materials and their relative sizes. When the galaxies do not collide, but come close enough for each galaxy's gravity to affect the other, they are described as interacting galaxies. As they get closer, the pull of gravity between them leads to their shape being pushed and pulled. Their interstellar gases may also be compressed, causing new waves of stars to be formed.

In about four billion years, the Milky Way and Andromeda galaxies will come together, with their flat discs of stars at an angle to each other.

COLLISION COURSE

While all galaxies are moving apart due to the expansion of the Universe, there is also a strong attraction pulling them together. This attraction is provided by the gravity of stars and black holes, as well as by the presence of vast amounts of dark matter. These combined forces can lead to collisions between galaxies. The Milky Way and Andromeda, for example, are currently travelling towards each other at a speed of around 420,000 km/h.

This image shows two colliding galaxies, 300 million light years away, during the slow process of merging into a single, giant galaxy. They are nicknamed 'the Mice' because of the long tails of stars and gas trailing from each galaxy.

WHEN GALAXIES CRASH

What happens when galaxies collide depends on their size, speed and the angle they meet at. A smaller galaxy might move through the disc of a larger galaxy and come out the other side, sending shockwaves of gravity that lead to new stars being created. Meanwhile, the larger galaxy might not change very much. Other clashes might lead to a new, irregular galaxy being formed.

iEXPLORE

CRASHING GALAXIES

Trigger an amazing video of two galaxies crashing together.

NEBULAE:
THE COSMIC LIGHTSHOW

'Space' suggests emptiness, but although the vast areas between the stars are close to being a total vacuum, they are not completely empty. Interstellar space still contains a very small amount of matter, as well as dark matter. This space is crossed by waves of light, other radiation and gravity. It is thought that the average density of the observable Universe is about the same as one hydrogen atom for every cubic metre. However, some of the least dense objects in the observable Universe are also among the largest and most colourful – the vast clouds of gas and dust found within galaxies that we call nebulae.

The Orion Nebula is one of the brightest emission nebulae. It is so large and bright that, from a dark site, it can be seen in the night sky without a telescope. The Orion Nebula is lit up by four massive stars at its centre.

BRIGHT NEBULAE

There are two types of bright, glowing nebulae. The first is an emission nebula. When a nebula is close to a young, very hot star, the radiation from that star can affect the hydrogen in the nebula's gas cloud, heating it up to almost 10,000°C. This energizes the hydrogen atoms, so that they start to emit light. Nebulae largely made of hydrogen tend to glow red, but if other elements are present they can also produce a greenish or blue light. The second type of bright nebula is a reflection nebula. This type is not close enough to a powerful star to absorb enough energy to create its own light. However, it is close enough for its microscopic dust particles to scatter the light from the star, reflecting it like a giant mirror. Reflection nebulae usually glow with a bluish colour.

This image of the Eagle Nebula shows a star-forming area known as the Pillars of Creation. New stars are formed within pillar-shaped clouds of hydrogen that are about five light years tall.

DYING STAR LIGHT

Planetary nebulae are fuzzy clouds that have rounded, planet-like shapes. They are created when a medium-sized star comes to the end of its life. As the star uses up its core of hydrogen, it swells up to become a red giant. Its cooler, outer layer detaches from the white-hot core and forms a roughly spherical nebula. Planetary nebulae glow with a variety of colours, their gases gathering energy to shine from the dying core of the star, known as a white dwarf. The death of a much more massive star can also leave behind a glowing supernova remnant, which forms a bright nebula.

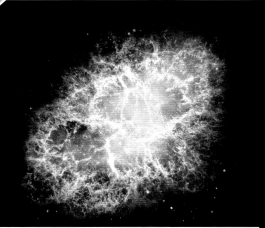

The supernova that created the Crab Nebula in 1054 AD was so bright that at first it was visible even in daytime and it could be seen in the night sky with the naked eye for about two years.

STELLAR NURSERIES

The low-density clouds that make up nebulae are the raw materials from which vastly denser stars can be made. These star nurseries often emit light and so are called emission nebulae. They are usually found in the discs of spiral galaxies. Nebulae that have been known for some time often have beautiful names, but recently discovered nebulae don't.

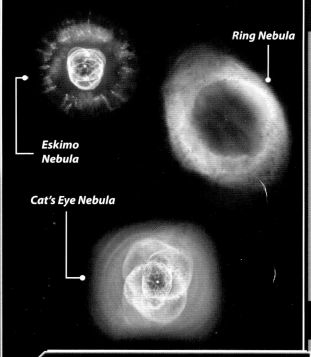

Ring Nebula

Eskimo Nebula

Cat's Eye Nebula

Planetary Nebulae produce an amazing array of colours in their shell of gases and can take a variety of shapes, as these examples show.

A STAR IS BORN

Stars are created from the clouds of gas and dust in nebulae, but they are not all born as equals. Depending on how much matter gathers and condenses to form them, the resulting stars can have very different futures. High-mass stars follow a separate life cycle from that of low-mass stars, and the end of their lives can be very different, too. Yet all stars begin the same way, with scattered gas, dust and the driving force of gravity.

In a process called accretion, a protostar is surrounded by the cocoon of gases that it is drawing into its dense core. As the mass and temperature of the core increases, the unstable protostar is ready for the next stage of its life cycle.

IN THE BEGINNING: PROTOSTARS

The life cycle of every star begins in darkness. Stars are created from the thin, cold clouds of gas and dust that form dark nebulae. It takes an immensely long time for the dispersed matter within these clouds to collapse into the super-dense balls of gas that become stars. It probably took 50 million years for our Sun to evolve into a bright, main sequence star. The process begins when gravity starts to concentrate regions of a dark nebula into denser cloud fragments. Each clump of matter becomes a gravitational centre, sucking in the gases around it. They form a swirling ball that gets hotter and denser at its centre, where gravity forces the matter smaller and smaller until it forms a dense core called a protostar. Over millions of years, more gas and dust is drawn into the protostar and it continues to grow, getting hotter and denser, hidden in the thick dust of the dark nebula.

iEXPLORE

STAR LIFE CYCLES

Swipe to select a pathway for your star's life cycle. It might end up as a white dwarf or a neutron star!

10 20 60

FAILED STARS

The future of a protostar is determined by the battle between the gravity that causes it to contract and the pressure created by the hot gases reacting at its core. If the protostar cannot gather enough mass, the pressure and temperature of the core will never get high enough to fire a thermonuclear reaction. This is why low-mass protostars fail to become main sequence stars. Instead, they turn into dimly glowing brown dwarfs, reddish in colour and often covered in clouds that mask their faint light.

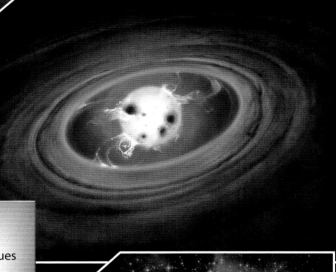

A brown dwarf looks similar to a gassy planet such as Jupiter, but it can be more than 75 times larger. Unlike a planet, a brown dwarf emits radiation. However, there is also a bright, light-generating layer beneath the clouds that creates dark bands on its surface.

As it moves towards the main sequence to become a true star, a young, unstable T Tauri star emits a jet of gases – known as a bipolar flow – from its poles.

A STAR IS BORN

In a more massive protostar, gravity continues to draw more and more hydrogen into its core. It therefore gets hotter, forming a violently unstable T Tauri star. At the core, heat breaks atoms up into charged particles, and wild magnetic fields and outflows cause violent flares. As the temperature and pressure build, the T Tauri star emits jets of hot gases from its poles, clearing away the cloud of gas and dust surrounding it. Finally, when the core reaches about 15,000,000°C, nuclear fusion is triggered – and a star begins its life.

A cluster of young main sequence stars in the constellation of Carina. The stars are surrounded by clouds of gas and dust – the remains of the nebula from which they formed.

SOLAR LEFTOVERS: THE PLANETS

The gas and dust cloud of a protostar collapses as a young star forms and becomes a flattened disc of matter rotating around it. Once a star enters the main sequence, the leftover materials form a protoplanetary disc that slowly cools and condenses into different elements. The stellar wind, created by the gases escaping the young star, pushes the lighter elements further out, leaving the denser materials closer to the star. The matter gradually forms itself into a system of planets in orbit around the star. In our Solar System, the denser materials clumped together to form rocky planets, while many of the lighter elements composed the gas giants.

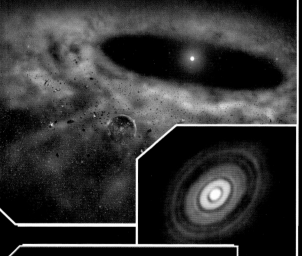

The matter in the disc surrounding a young star slowly separates out into bands. These eventually pull together to form individual planets from the gas and dust within each band. This image shows the young star HL Tau and the bands of its protoplanetary disc.

DYING STARS

As long as there's hydrogen to fuel the nuclear reactions within its core, a main sequence star can create enough outward pressure to balance the forces of gravity trying to squash it. About 90 per cent of a star's life is spent as a stable, main sequence star, but as the fuel runs out, it enters the final phases of its existence. The end of a dying star is decided by its mass. Star deaths range from a slow fading-away to a very sudden, explosive ending.

Around 90 per cent of the stars in the observable Universe are main sequence stars. Sirius A, the brightest star in the night sky, is just under nine light years away from Earth and is a main sequence star like our Sun.

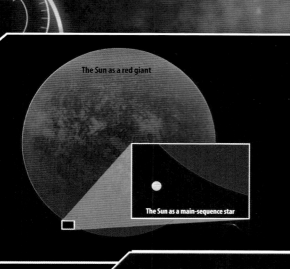

The Sun as a red giant

The Sun as a main-sequence star

Our Sun is a medium-sized main sequence star, about halfway through its life. It will probably be stable for another four billion years, before it slowly grows into a red giant.

THE END OF A SUN

G-98

Once a medium-sized star has turned all the hydrogen in its core into helium, its nuclear reactions cease. The core collapses and gets even hotter. This heat expands the outer gas shell of the star, which gets cooler and redder. Meanwhile, the renewed heat from the core kicks off the fusion of hydrogen in the gas shell. The burning moves further out, as the hydrogen in the outer layers gets used up, and the star swells to become a red giant. The core eventually gets hot enough to fuse its helium into carbon, while the outer layers detach and form a planetary nebula. After this dying burst of energy, the star becomes a glowing white dwarf, slowly cooling over billions of years, before fading away as a black dwarf.

THE SLOW FATE OF LOW-MASS STARS

During their main sequence phase, low-mass stars consume hydrogen much more slowly. This means that they can shine for hundreds of billions of years, but they are cooler and much less bright than Sun-like stars. When their core hydrogen runs out, they start using the hydrogen in their outer layers. However, they cannot generate enough heat or pressure at their core to use helium as an alternative fuel, when the hydrogen runs out completely. After expanding for a while, they collapse, get smaller, and finally turn into very dim black dwarfs.

Proxima Centauri is the nearest known star to the Sun, but it is a low-mass red dwarf star, too dim to be seen with the naked eye at night. Low-mass red dwarfs are the most common stars in the Milky Way.

Betelgeuse is a red supergiant, 1,000 times larger than the Sun and 100,000 times brighter. It is an old star, close to the end of its life, and because of its colossal mass is likely to explode as a supernova within a million years.

iEXPLORE

RELEASE A BLACK HOLE

Trigger a black hole in your bedroom!

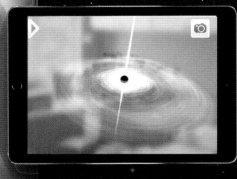

DEATH OF A GIANT

With so much hydrogen available to them, high-mass stars burn fiercely with a blue light that can be more than a million times brighter than the Sun. Such stars are vast, up to ten times broader than our Sun, but their size and larger fuel reserves do not enable them to live for longer. A larger star's core needs to create energy more rapidly to maintain a balance against the much greater force of gravity pushing inwards. The star has more hydrogen, but it has to use it up quickly.

When its hydrogen has been used up, a high-mass star expands to form a red supergiant, burning the hydrogen in its outer shell until the star collapses. The temperature created in the core can fuse the helium into carbon, and it can also do the same with a series of heavier elements produced in turn – until the core finally turns to iron and no more fusion can occur. Gravity then collapses the core in less than a second. Its temperature rises to 10,000,000,000°C, breaking up the iron nuclei in the core into small particles and triggering a huge burst of light and energy known as a type II supernova which may turn into a black hole.

GOING SUPERNOVA:
NEUTRON STARS AND BLACK HOLES

The fate of most stars – about 95 per cent – is to end as a white dwarf, glowing with their remaining energy until they slowly fade to darkness. But the fate of massive stars is to go out with a bang. When a massive star dies, it collapses inwards, triggering a supernova – an immense explosion of energy and light. Brighter than the light of billions of suns, this dying burst of energy can last for months, outshining everything in the galaxy surrounding it.

Following the final collapse of a massive star that triggers a colossal supernova explosion, a neutron star or a black hole may be created.

SPECTACULAR SUPERNOVAE

There are two main types of supernova. The first is created in a binary star system, where a white dwarf star and a giant star orbit around the same point in space. The smaller star starts to suck in material from its larger companion, until the white dwarf becomes unstable and explodes as a type I supernova. A type II supernova happens at the end of a massive star's solo life, when it has run out of fuel and can no longer prevent its core from collapsing under the pressure of gravity.

AFTERMATH

A supernova event creates a shockwave that carries star debris into space, creating a shell-like cloud around it. This gas-and-dust shell contains heavier elements forged in the heart of the star. Most of the Universe is made of simple elements such as hydrogen and helium, so supernovae play a key role in scattering more complex elements, such as metals, around the Universe. They inject these elements into the interstellar medium, where they become part of the mix from which new stars and planets can be formed. Earth itself contains elements forged in the cores of one or more large, dying stars.

The Crab Nebula is a supernova remnant – an expanding shell of gas and dust created by the supernova of a dying massive star. This cloud of stellar debris may help to create new stars.

We cannot see black holes but they can be detected by how they affect other objects. They might bend light from nearby stars, cause wobbles in the movement of stars or planets, or even drag giant stars into themselves.

BLACK HOLES

When a massive star – one with a mass greater than three times that of the Sun – explodes in a supernova, the remnants of its core continue to collapse, until all its matter has been compressed into a single point of incredible density, known as a singularity. This dense concentration of mass creates a powerful gravitational field around it, so powerful that even light cannot escape its pull. The dark void of a black hole is surrounded by a whirlpool of stars, gas and dust, all of which are being drawn into its vortex of gravity. This disc of matter, called an accretion disc, makes the edges of the black hole visible, a boundary known as the event horizon. Once anything passes that boundary, it disappears. What happens beyond that point is unknown.

Less than 20 km across, a neutron star contains twice the mass of the Sun. About 2,000 neutron stars are said to be in the Milky Way and the Magellanic Clouds.

NEUTRON STARS AND PULSARS

A star at the lower end of the massive scale is between one-and-a-half and three times the mass of our Sun. After a type II supernova, the core of such a star (having shed its outer layers) collapses further under gravity. The atoms in the core are squashed until they form smaller particles called neutrons, all tightly packed into the smallest and most dense type of star – a neutron star. Once formed, a neutron star continues to rotate rapidly. Its strong magnetic fields can lead to beams of radiation being fired from its poles. These beams, combined with the spinning, can create pulses of radio waves. Neutron stars that do this are called pulsars.

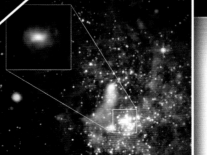

Sagittarius A* is the supermassive black hole at the centre of the Milky Way.

SUPERMASSIVE BLACK HOLES

Black holes grow by drawing in more mass, absorbing the stars, gas and dust around them. They can also expand by merging with other black holes to form a supermassive black hole. The black hole at the heart of our galaxy, the Milky Way, is almost four million times the mass of the Sun.

THE END OF THE UNIVERSE

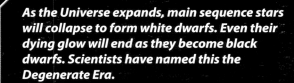

As the Universe expands, main sequence stars will collapse to form white dwarfs. Even their dying glow will end as they become black dwarfs. Scientists have named this the Degenerate Era.

The story of the Universe is still unfolding. We know that space is still expanding. So, what happens next? As we have seen, stars are born, live and die. Gravity and expasion seem to control the whole Universe, which suggests that it may also end one day. But do we know how? Here are some ideas.

ENDLESS EXPANSION

Today's Universe is still fairly young. At this stage of its life, stars and galaxies can exist – but this period of starlight cannot last for ever. The expansion of the Universe is speeding up at its most distant edges, under the influence of dark energy. With dark energy overcoming gravity, galaxies and stars are no longer being held together and will spread out into ever-expanding space. This is the most likely fate of the Universe – endless expansion, in which everything will drift further and further apart.

THE BIG FREEZE

As the expansion of space goes on, the Universe will get colder and darker. Stars and galaxies will continue to lose energy as the matter they are made from breaks up and becomes more disordered. Eventually, more than a trillion years from now, all the main sequence stars will have consumed their fuel, fading away to become black dwarfs, while the high-mass stars will have collapsed to form neutron stars and black holes. The dying glow of starlight will be followed by darkness, when matter itself will be broken up into its smallest particles. Finally, the Universe will take on a frozen, lightless state known as the Big Freeze.

iEXPLORE

LIGHT SPECTRUMS

View the night sky from Earth in 360° and select telescopic close-up views using different light spectrums to look at a distant galaxy.